WELCOME TO THE FARM

1 Combine Harvester

Samantha Bell

Published in the United States of America
by Cherry Lake Publishing
Ann Arbor, Michigan
www.cherrylakepublishing.com

Content Adviser: Gary Powell, Weed Science Research Technician,
Michigan State University
Reading Adviser: Marla Conn MS, Ed., Literacy specialist, Read-Ability, Inc.
Photo Credits: © AGCO Corporation, all rights reserved, cover, 1, 2;
© TTstudio/Shutterstock, 4; © Fotokostic/Shutterstock, 6, 8;
© moglimoglzahn/Shutterstock, 10; © Stefan Kunchev Kunchev/Shutterstock, 12;
© Henry Nowick/Shutterstock, 14; © Edler von Rabenstein/Shutterstock, 16;
© smereka/Shutterstock, 18; © auremar/Shutterstock, 20

Library of Congress Cataloging-in-Publication Data
Names: Bell, Samantha, author. | Bell, Samantha. Welcome to the farm.
Title: Combine harvester / Samantha Bell.
Description: Ann Arbor : Cherry Lake Publishing, [2016] | Series: Welcome to
  the farm | Includes bibliographical references and index.
Identifiers: LCCN 2015047225| ISBN 9781634710343 (hardcover) |
  ISBN 9781634711333 (pdf) | ISBN 9781634712323 (pbk.) |
  ISBN 9781634713313 (ebook)
Subjects: LCSH: Combines (Agricultural machinery)—Juvenile literature.
Classification: LCC S696 .B44 2016 | DDC 631.3/7—dc23
LC record available at http://lccn.loc.gov/2015047225

Cherry Lake Publishing would like to acknowledge the work of the Partnership
for 21st Century Skills. Please visit www.p21.org for more information.

Printed in the United States of America
Corporate Graphics

Table of Contents

What things does grain need to grow?

The Grain is Ready

Some farmers grow **grain**. Combines help **harvest** grain.

A combine harvester does three jobs. It cuts the **crop**. It **threshes** the grain from the crop. It cleans and delivers the grain to the combine grain bin.

The Header

The header is on the front. It moves the crop into the combine. This one is for harvesting corn.

A cutter bar cuts the **stalks**. This one is for cutting wheat.

The Threshing Drum

The plants go to the threshing drum. The drum beats the plants.

What does grain feel like to touch?

The grain falls off the stalks.

The Tank

A tank holds the grain.
The stalks fall on the
ground.

The tank is full. A truck takes the grain away.

Time to gather another crop!

Find Out More

Gabel, Stacey. *It's Time to Combine*. Indianapolis: Dog Ear Publishing, 2009.

Claas Lexion Combine
http://app.claas.com/2012/lexion/3d-standalone/us/
View a combine from all sides.

Glossary

crop (KRAHP) a plant that is grown as food or for other uses
grain (GRAYN) cereal plants such as barley, oats, wheat, and rye
harvest (HAHR-vist) to gather crops
stalks (STAWKS) plant stems
threshes (THRESH-ez) separates the grain or seed from a cereal plant such as wheat by beating

Home and School Connection

Use this list of words from the book to help your child become a better reader. Word games and writing activities can help beginning readers reinforce literacy skills.

and	delivers	ground	moves	this
another	does	grow	need	three
away	drum	harvest	off	threshes
bar	falls	harvester	on	threshing
beats	farmers	harvesting	one	time
bin	feel	header	plants	to
cleans	for	help	ready	touch
combines	from	holds	some	truck
corn	front	into	stalks	what
crop	full	is	takes	wheat
cuts	gather	it	tank	
cutter	go	jobs	the	
cutting	grain	like	things	

Index

About the Author

Samantha Bell is a children's book writer, illustrator, teacher, and mom of four busy kids. Her articles, short stories, and poems have been published online and in print.